THE PRODIGAL HUGGING CHURCH

A Scandalous Approach to Mission for the 21st Century

TIM WRIGHT

JoyResources

To B.J. and Gloria,
What a difference you've made in my life!
I'm honored to call you friends.

Contents

I am an older brother.
I am the first born of five children.
I have all of the stereotypical qualities of the older sibling.
I'm:
perfectionistic,
legalistic, and
concerned about what's fair, just, and right.
I'm quite self-sufficient,
and have a hard time tolerating those who aren't.
At times I can be very judgmental
toward those who don't get it right or
toward those who don't measure up to my standards.
Particularly toward those pesky younger siblings
who always seem to get away with it.
I'm also a prodigal.
My need for perfection always leaves me short.
I crave:
unconditional acceptance,
love,
and freedom from always having to do it right.
I yearn for God's grace.
These two sides of me don't always get along.

—TIM WRIGHT

Preface

Ever since the second grade I have dreamed of serving as a pastor in an innovative ministry committed to reaching the community with the love of Christ. That dream became a reality in March 1982 when I visited Community Church of Joy in Glendale, Arizona, for the first time. My wife, Jan, and I flew down to the Phoenix area to meet with the staff of Joy prior to my assignment as an intern pastor there beginning in August. I immediately fell in love with the city, the community, and the church. The passion of Joy to build a church for those who don't go to church tapped into my lifelong call.

I have been a part of Joy since then, serving as one of the pastors since April 1984. In that time I have had the chance to work with a congregation of people bold enough to do whatever it takes to impact culture with the life-changing message of Jesus. Innovation, creativity, and risk, for the sake of the gospel, drive this particular mission. I love this place!

Because Joy has gained a reputation as a teaching congregation, I've had the chance to meet many innovative leaders from various denominations, cultural settings, and church sizes—leaders, both clergy and lay, who have a dream burning in their bellies to do something creative to engage the culture outside of their churches. They dare to try new things to reach new people. Yet many of these leaders find the door slammed in their faces again and again by those who believe that church is primarily for church people. Worship wars, culture wars, withheld giving, threatened splits, and power struggles continually eat away at their desire to pursue the mission God has called them to, leaving them discouraged and frustrated.

I understand the frustration. Because Joy has been a church committed to those not connected to the church, because we seek to connect with culture in relevant ways, we've had our share of critics both internally and externally. Sometimes the criticism has been vicious, personal, and cruel. And quite honestly, there have been times in my ministry when, in the face of the criticisms, I've questioned my call and the mission of Joy.

A few years ago, I was beginning to work on a lecture for an upcoming major conference Joy was hosting. The key text for the lecture was the story of the prodigal son in Luke 15. As I reflected on the story, it dawned on me that Jesus faced similar challenges. His innovative ministry to those outside of religious culture was constantly criticized by those inside the religious world (just as the older brother in the story had no time for the prodigal). Yet Jesus was very clear about his mission in spite of the criticism—he came to embrace prodigals on God's behalf. Out of that experience grew the concept of the Prodigal Hugging Church. Prodigal Hugging Churches do what Jesus does—they embrace the prodigals of their communities. Often their mission to the culture outside of the church is criticized and misunderstood, as was true for Jesus, but for the sake of the gospel they keep at it.

> "The Son of Man came to look for and to save people who are lost."
>
> —Jesus
>
> (Luke 19:10 CEV)

This book is written to encourage the leaders and members of Prodigal Hugging Churches to keep up the good work. It offers that encouragement through my own personal experience, along with stories, scriptures, examples, and practical insights into how to make the church more culture-friendly. This book also serves as an invitation for all believers to rethink the mission of their congregations in light of Jesus' commitment to embrace culture.

So get your hugging arms ready. God invites us to an adventure that can change our lives, our ministries, and our communities.

Culture Encounter 1

Trivia Question: What is the highest rated TV sport in the United States? Professional Football?. . . Baseball?. . . Basketball? You might be surprised to learn that the answer is . . . Pro Wrestling! (And in the case of Pro Wrestling, I use the term "sport" loosely.) My teenage son put me on to this phenomenon a few years ago. He and his friends get together every week to watch their favorite wrestling heroes take part in struggles between good and evil. And my son and his friends are not alone. Professional Wrestling has captured the hearts and imaginations of a large portion of our population—specifically males ages 15 to 30.

Some time ago, my brother Jeff and I stood in line to buy our kids tickets to an upcoming World Championship Wrestling (WCW) event. As I looked at all the young people waiting in line with us, I wondered how we could reach them with the love of Christ. About that time, I came across a book in a Christian bookstore called *Every Man Has His Price*, the autobiography of Ted DiBiase. Ted wrestled as "The Million Dollar Man" for the World Wrestling Federation (WWF). My son, Mike, hates reading, but I thought he might try this book. And he did. He devoured it in a couple of days. In fact, he was so excited about the book that he begged me to bring Ted to our church to share his story.

So I invited Ted to be part of our Sunday morning worship experience. Instead of doing our regular service, we opted that day to use a talk show format—to build the Sunday experience around special music from the band and an extended interview with Ted. No sermon. No Bible reading. No worship. Just Ted and I talking together.

We promoted the event for several weeks and it paid off. That Sunday morning the place was jammed. To our delight, we had a lot of young people in the audience. We started the service with a nice, up-tempo song by the band. I followed up by welcoming everyone to Community Church of Joy and our Sunday service as I usually do, and then had them stand and greet each other. As they took their seats, I explained that this particular service would be unique from what we typically do on Sunday morning. But as I spoke, my brother Jeff mumbled into a microphone, "I still think you're wrong."

I turned, looked at him, and then continued talking to the audience. Jeff interrupted me again. "I'm serious, I still think you're wrong."

I said, "Look, Jeff, we're trying to do a service here. We'll settle this later." But Jeff wouldn't let it go. He said, "I want to settle it right now."

So I turned to the audience and explained, "Jeff and I had a bit of a disagreement right before the service and apparently he needs to take care of it immediately. I really apologize for this, but if you'd hang in there with us for just one moment, we'll be right back." And with that we walked off the stage.

Seconds later, a video came up on the screen with the two of us walking into a wrestling ring. For the next three minutes we held a wrestling match, choreographed by my son, Mike. We did several famous wrestling moves (poorly) and finally I maneuvered my way into Ted DiBiase's patented sleeper hold on Jeff. With Jeff at my mercy, I said, "Do you give?"

Jeff replied, "Yah. I give."

"Then say it."

"No. I don't want to say it."

"Say it!" I demanded.

After a pause, Jeff said, "Barry Manilow is better than Boston."

"Louder!"

"Barry Manilow is better than Boston."

And with that, Jeff fell to the mat fast asleep. With arms in the air, I said, "I knew he'd see it my way."

After the video, I walked back on stage and introduced Ted. The guys in the band played his theme music as he walked out and Ted gave his signature laugh. The two of us sat on a couple of chairs while I asked him questions about wrestling in general and about his own career. Ten minutes into the interview, we took a break and the band did another song. Then Ted and I returned to the stage where the conversation shifted to his encounter with Christ. Ted told of how empty his life had been even though to make his "Million Dollar Man" character credible, he lived the million-dollar lifestyle courtesy of the WWF. He then shared how, through the love of his wife, he discovered the love of Christ. Tears filled his eyes as he spoke.

At that moment something "magical" happened. God's Spirit took over. As Ted told his story the room fell silent. You could have heard the proverbial pin drop on the carpeted floor. People sat riveted as the Spirit touched their hearts through Ted's words. It was one of those special times when you could feel God at work in the moment. We closed the interview with a time of prayer for those who needed a fresh start with God. The band tied it all together with a great song about how God loves us as we are.

That service was one of the most spiritually profound worship experiences I've been a part of in more than fifteen years at Community Church of Joy, even though it looked more like a late-night talk show than a worship service. For two hours after the service, Ted autographed his book for all the kids, big and small, who wanted to meet him. Ted's book provided yet another chance for people to hear about the life-transforming love of Jesus. It was a great day.

But there was another, equally significant response to that event.

After the service I asked my daughter, Alycia, who is not a wrestling fan, what she thought about the service. She gave it two thumbs up. She then proceeded to tell me about the reaction of two of the people sitting behind her during the service. She said that throughout the service they were complaining—out loud. They were flabbergasted that we had a wrestler on stage. They were upset because we weren't singing praises to Jesus or preaching from the Bible. They simply could not believe we were doing such a thing and calling it church. They were outraged.

Culture Challenges

I regularly receive calls from pastors with questions about ministry. They bounce ideas off me or share some of their pain and frustration as they seek to move their congregations in a new, mission-oriented direction. Three recent calls from three different pastors capture the heart and essence of what I usually hear. All three pastors accepted a call to small, established congregations. All three entered their new churches with high hopes and big dreams. During the interview process, all three shared their visions for building mission-focused, outreach-oriented congregations. And all three congregations reflected back to the candidates their desires for such a mission and vision. All three churches longed for a new direction and a fresh connection with the community. The match looked perfect in all three cases.

"Healthy people don't need a doctor, but sick people do. I didn't come to invite good people to be my followers. I came to invite sinners."

—Jesus
(Mark 2:17 CEV)

The first pastor, after five years in his church, not only resigned his position, but also dropped out of the ministry. He couldn't take the pain and viciousness of "church people" anymore. The second pastor lasted one and one-half years before he came to the conclusion that he no longer wanted to run up against brick walls. He put his name in for a new call and eventually changed denominations.

The third pastor has been through the war with his church. The pain and frustration has taken its toll on him and his congregation. Some long-time members left. Others stayed, hoping that the church would come to its senses and get back to business as usual. But the church is growing. New families are joining the congregation as a result of the new, innovative approach to mission and worship adopted by the congregation. This church, out of the three, will make it to the dream and vision that the pastor and the congregation agreed to. But the process hasn't come without a price. While the pastor certainly celebrates the new things God is doing, the tears of two years of frustration and hard-fought battles come easily as he recounts the path from the old to the new.

Admittedly, a whole host of reasons exist as to why conflict happens in a church—the dynamics of change, the wrong fit between pastor and congregation, the old guard versus the new guard, the right vision but the wrong church, and so on. Increasingly, however, I'm convinced that another dynamic lies behind the battles and struggles—a dynamic we don't often talk about. That dynamic can be summarized by the following questions: *To what extent will we allow culture to impact our mission?* (By *culture* I mean everything outside of the church: the people, the language, the music, the technology, the beliefs and traditions, and so on—everything the church might label as "secular culture.") *How much of culture will we allow in the church? How much of culture will we use? How much like culture will we become before there's no difference between the rest of the world and us? Where do we draw the line between the church and culture?*

Culture

The ideas, customs, skills, and arts of a given people at a given time.

In my opinion, one of the major causes of conflict in churches today is not the issue of whether or not we should reach out to the community. Most believers admit, even if it's begrudgingly, that that's what the church is called to do. The conflict is not so much about hospitality and making the church more visitor-friendly to outsiders. We all buy into that, even the most inhospitable among us. The cause behind much of the chaos in churches and the reason why many congregations fail in their attempts at innovative mission is the practical application of mission itself. In other words, the bottom-line reason behind many of the headaches in churches today, and my congregation is no exception, is the relationship between church and culture—the extent to which outside culture should dictate the mission of the church and how close to culture the church ought to get.

Not that we should find this surprising. The tension over the relationship between Church and culture has been a part of Christian history since the creation of the Church.

To Be In . . . or Not to Be In

For the last two thousand years, the Christian Church has seemingly had a love/hate relationship with culture. On the one hand, we know that Jesus invites us as his followers to go into culture and make disciples of all peoples. He calls us to be in the world in order to share his life-transforming love with others.

On the other hand, as people transformed by the love of Christ, we want to align ourselves with his values and increasingly distance ourselves from the impact of the negative values of culture. Although Jesus calls us into the world, the apostle Paul warns us not to conform to culture—or not to be of the world.

My sense is that over the last two thousand years church-goers have focused more on the *be not of the world* than we have on the *be in the world* part of the Christian life. Our history tends to be that of withdrawal and isolation from culture, domination of culture (as in the Crusades), boycotting of culture, and criticizing of culture. And for good reason. Culture so often seems to embrace anti-God values that can enslave and destroy. So to protect ourselves from culture's negative values and to model what we hope reflects the life-affirming values of the kingdom of God, we withdraw from culture and create our own subculture. We do so by adamantly resisting the encroachment of culture into our worship services, particularly in the area of music. In our new subculture, we choose music that the culture at large rarely, if ever, listens to or understands. We create our own traditions, which stand in stark contrast to the traditions of the world. We use "religious" language that only "insiders" get. We build religious buildings, display religious symbols, and wear religious clothing, all of which usually looks very different from anything else in culture.

In our attempt to take seriously the biblical imperative not to be conformed to the world, we as Christians have created a new culture that only believers seem to understand. And then, when we invite people from secular society into our churches, we wonder why they don't understand or appreciate our God-centered culture. We can't figure out why they feel lost and alienated. It must be their problem.

Again, as Christians we know we need to tap into wider culture to share the love of Christ. At the same time, as a people called to be holy by a holy God, we want to make sure that we don't compromise with, condone, or become too much like the culture we're called to reach. Finding the balance between tapping into mass culture and yet staying true to the values of the Christian life has not been easy for us.

How we deal with the issue of culture is vitally important because how we see our relationship with culture has everything to do with who we are as a church, what our mission is, and how effective we'll be in reaching culture. If we become too isolated from or antagonistic toward what is happening outside of the church, we risk losing any voice in the wider culture. The rest of society will simply turn us off. If we become too identified with mass culture, we run the risk of having nothing better to offer people than what culture already has.

So how do we build a culture-friendly church without compromising our values as Christians? How do we walk that fine line between "being in" but not "being of" the world in such a way that culture can clearly see the relevance and radical difference of the gospel? How do we take the message of the kingdom of God and make it accessible to the rest of society?

A Scandalous Approach to Culture

I'd like to suggest that Jesus provides the answers to these all-important questions. Throughout his ministry Jesus modeled an approach to culture that can revolutionize our congregations—a model that can revitalize our sense of mission and our ability to reconnect with a culture that so desperately needs to hear about him. It needs to be said up front, however, that his approach to culture is filled with risks and dangers—risks and dangers Jesus was willing to face for the sake of culture, and risks we must be willing to face as well.

Perhaps the best "apologetic" for Jesus' relationship with culture and his approach to reaching it is recorded in Luke 15—the "lost and found" chapter.

In Luke 15, Jesus finds himself confronted by the religious leaders of his day. As usual, they were upset with him. They criticized him because he constantly surrounded himself with what they considered to be the low life of society—people like despised tax collectors, filthy prostitutes, and non-religious sinners. You can almost hear the Pharisees sniff in condescension as they complain, "This fellow welcomes sinners and eats with them."

In essence, the Pharisees were saying, "This fellow is too close to culture. He welcomes sinners and hangs with them. He calls them his friends. He even acts like them. He parties too much. He drinks too much. How can he possibly call himself a religious leader when he looks, acts, and smells so much like common sinners? This man has disqualified himself from leadership." In other words, the religious leaders found Jesus' identification with the rest of society scandalous.

"Father, I don't ask you to take my followers out of the world, but keep them safe from the evil one. They don't belong to this world, and neither do I. Your word is truth. So let this truth make them completely yours. I am sending them into the world, just as you sent me."

—Jesus

(John 17:15-18 CEV)

To better comprehend their indignation, we need to understand the Pharisees' philosophy of God and culture. The Pharisees believed that God wanted nothing to do with the non-religious and sinners. The Pharisees assumed that God cared only about those who believed in God like they did. And believing that God shunned "sinners," they did likewise.

A couple of years ago, Joy's Leadership Center hosted a conference at Walt Disney World. During the event, one of our band members found himself engaged in a conversation with an employee of the hotel where we were staying. The employee asked him what brought him to Walt Disney World. When he told her he was playing drums for a church conference, the woman was intrigued, particularly since so many churches were boycotting the Disney Company. The conversation quickly turned to faith. The woman shared that her daughter had become pregnant outside of marriage. After the baby was born, the new mom called a local Lutheran church to ask if she could have her child baptized. The pastor said, "We don't take people off the streets!"

The Pharisees had a similar attitude toward culture. Believing that God was anti-culture, the Pharisees shunned the wider culture. And they criticized and condemned anyone who got too close to culture, like Jesus. Jesus, however, had a very different view of God's attitude toward culture. And to share that view, and at the same time to respond to the Pharisees' complaint, Jesus did what he often did—he told a story. The story shares God's heart for mission and how God chooses to respond to culture in order to carry out that mission.

Scandal
Unseemly conduct of a religious person that discredits religion.

Scandalize
To offend by some improper or unconventional behavior.

Scandalous
Offensive to a sense of decency or shocking to the moral feelings of a community.

A Story about a Lost Son

The story focuses on a father and his two sons: One day the younger son came to his father and asked for his share of the inheritance early . . .

Those listening to Jesus' story, upon hearing the younger son's request, no doubt responded with a collective gasp. They knew that the act of asking for one's inheritance early was absolutely scandalous. By making such a request, the younger son devalued his father and his father's authority—bringing public disgrace on his father . . .

The father gave his younger son the money, and immediately the younger son headed off to a distant country where he used his money for less than noble purposes. To put it succinctly, he squandered his inheritance on wild living (you can use your own imagination as to what that means). The son eventually ran out of money. And as luck would have it, a deep recession hit the country at the same time. Destitute and all alone, he finally landed a job feeding pigs . . .

Another audible gasp! Jewish law forbids any kind of contact with unclean pigs. To lower oneself to feed them meant that the younger son had gone past the point of no return. He was lost. There was no hope for him. He was beyond redemption . . .

One day, while feeding the pigs and feeling extremely hungry himself, the younger son realized that these pigs were living better than he was. So he swallowed his pride and decided to go back to his father and beg for forgiveness. He would declare himself unworthy of being a son and would return home only if his father would treat him as a hired hand.

After the long journey home, the younger son rounded that familiar corner where his house came into view. To his surprise, he saw his father standing at the end of the drive. As soon as the father saw his younger son, he lifted his robes and started running toward him. The father was filled with compassion for his son. When the father reached his son, he threw his arms around him and hugged him. Although his son had hurt him deeply, the father welcomed his son back home and celebrated his return with a huge party.

But there was another, equally significant response to the prodigal. The older brother, hearing about the reception his younger brother had received, was absolutely incensed. In fact, he was scandalized, and for good reason. As mentioned, his brother had completely disqualified himself from the family and from any kind of acceptance through his scandalous behavior. He had:

✓ humiliated the family by asking for his inheritance early;

✓ wasted his money on wild living; and

✓ worked on a pig farm.

Three strikes. He's out!

But the actions of his father also scandalized him, perhaps even more so. First, his father threw a party for this son who had so humiliated the family, making a mockery out of all that is right, just, proper, and fair. The older son couldn't possibly understand why his father would hug someone who had so deeply disappointed him. Second, his father had lifted his robes and had run to the younger son. In Jesus' day, an elderly man shamed himself if he lifted his robes and ran in public.

Considering all of the above, one can understand why the older brother was so upset. Everything about his prodigal brother and his forgiving father was scandalous. He had every right to be angry, at least from his perspective.

God's Approach to Culture

To understand the point of the story, we need to remember what prompted its telling in the first place. Jesus told the story in response to the criticism from the religious leaders that he was too cozy with the questionable people in society. Jesus used the story to explain his behavior and to clarify God's radical approach to culture.

With that in mind, the point of the story is this: God cares deeply about the lost sons and daughters of the world—about those prodigals who don't know him. God's heart yearns to reach them and to offer them something that can heal them and make them new. And God's strategy for reaching culture is absolutely astounding: God, in the person of Jesus, decided to become like culture. He became like the people he wants to find—so that he can put his arms around them, affirm them, welcome them, and ultimately lead them home.

To put it another way, the mission of Jesus is to climb into culture and hug prodigals so he might transform them. Jesus joyfully lifts his robes and runs to prodigals—he scandalizes himself—in order to hug them. And he calls us as his Church to develop a similar attitude—to reach out to culture with that same kind of loving, reckless abandon; to risk scandal by immersing ourselves in culture and hugging prodigals, that the people of culture might be transformed. God invites us to become Prodigal Hugging Churches.

Culture Encounter 2

In 1992, Whoopi Goldberg starred in *Sister Act,* one of the best church-growth movies ever made. In the film, Whoopi Goldberg plays a lounge singer on the run from the "bad guys." The police hide her in a convent attached to an inner-city church and change her name to Sister Mary Clarence. In the convent, Sister Mary Clarence quickly discovers that the choir can't sing, the worship services put people to sleep, and, as a result, hardly anyone comes to church. She ends up taking over the choir and revitalizes it along with the worship service.

During her first Sunday as the choir director, Sister Mary Clarence leads the choir in a very traditional hymn. After a brief pause, the choir breaks into a pop version of the song complete with a few dance moves choreographed by Sister Mary Clarence. People standing outside the church hear the music and come in. When the song is over, the congregation applauds, and Sister Mary Clarence turns to them and smiles . . . until her eyes meet the icy stare of the Reverend Mother.

In the next scene, the Reverend Mother chews out Sister Mary Clarence. She demands to know why Sister Mary Clarence used that "boogie woogie" music in church. Sister Mary Clarence explains that she was trying to make the service more "Vegas-like" in the hope of getting more people into church. She's convinced that people stay away from church because it's a drag. At the same time, she believes that if the church could offer a service that has the energy of a casino or a theater they could pack the sanctuary.

"Through blasphemy?" asks the Reverend Mother. "You have corrupted the entire choir."

The Characteristics of a Prodigal Hugging Church

Prodigal Hugging Churches boldly return to the mission-driven, culture-friendly ministry of Jesus in order to impact the world today. They lay aside reputation and self-serving agendas that they might reach those who don't yet know Jesus. They choose people over programs and scandal over propriety for the sake of the gospel. Taking their cue from Jesus, they internalize and live out the seven following characteristics.

1. Prodigal Hugging Churches Embrace Culture (John 1:1-14)

The Word became a human being and lived here with us.
(John 1:14 CEV)

To *embrace* means to clasp in the arms, to show affection toward, to cherish and love, to offer acceptance. That's exactly what God did for us in Jesus. He embraced us by becoming like us. Where the religious leaders of Jesus' day chose to withdraw from culture, God, in the person of Jesus, chose to embrace it.

What's remarkable about Jesus is just how much he identified with culture. He looked like the people of his day. He dressed like them. He ate the same food they did. He used their language. He hung out at parties with all kinds of "undesirable" people. As a result, the religious leaders condemned him because they failed— or refused—to see beyond the external.

Yet Jesus was very different from culture—and the prodigals he spent time with knew it. Although he looked like the people of his day, Jesus had a unique internal compass. His values and principles were forged in a much different furnace than were the values and principles of those he was trying to reach. The message he preached had a fresh ring of authenticity and transformation to it. People could see and hear it. Jesus marched to a different drummer. Jesus was motivated by something attractive and inviting—something that offered hope to the lost and broken. In essence, Jesus was both totally in the world, and at the same time, totally not of the world.

To put it another way, *The kingdom of God is radically different from culture. But the ruler of that kingdom became radically like culture in order to embrace it.*

The Incarnation clearly demonstrates that God approaches culture by permeating the secular with the sacred and the sacred with the secular. Unfortunately, we in the Church tend to build walls to separate the two. Prodigal Hugging Churches seek to do what Jesus does and remove the walls by embracing culture.

What does it mean for the Church to embrace culture in order to reach it? How far are you and your congregation willing to go to take on the form of culture? To look like culture? To smell like culture? To speak like culture?

A few years ago, a man who looked to be in his late sixties came up to me after a worship service. He was wearing a plaid, short-sleeved polo shirt, striped shorts, black socks, and dress shoes. He grabbed me by the shirt and said, in all seriousness, "I am deeply offended by your clothing." I was wearing a nice shirt, a Mickey Mouse tie, black pants, and white Reeboks shoes, because I want my clothing to reflect the culture we're trying to reach. This man said, "I find your choice of wearing a tie with tennis shoes to be totally inappropriate for church."

I playfully grabbed his shirt and said, "First of all, if you had worn that outfit to the church I attended as a kid, you would have been thrown out. Secondly, what I'm wearing is perfectly normal. Reeboks are the dress shoes of my generation."

He shook his head apologetically and said, "I'm really out of the loop, aren't I?"

Although this is a simple story on the face of it, it pictures the profound undercurrents within the church.

What are the unwritten rules in your church that keep out prodigals? For example, what is the unwritten dress code? What is the assumed spiritual language in your worship service? What is the assumed level of spirituality in your discipleship ministry?

To take it a step further, what is your congregation willing to embrace by way of language, music, and clothing in order to hug prodigals, knowing that you risk offending many others in your congregation? How will you immerse yourself in culture while at the same time clearly demonstrating the counter-cultural values of God's kingdom?

I've said to our staff, somewhat overstated to make the point but true to the spirit of embracing culture: "The more we look like culture, and the less we look like a church, the more effective we'll be in reaching culture." How will your congregation choose to embrace culture?

2. Prodigal Hugging Churches Welcome Culture (John 4)

Jesus asked her, "Would you please give me a drink of water?"
"You are a Jew," she replied, "and I am a Samaritan woman. How
can you ask me for a drink of water when Jews and Samaritans
won't have anything to do with each other?" (John 4:8 9 CEV)

To *welcome* means to receive gladly into one's presence or companionship. Much to the chagrin of the religious leaders of his day, who refused to get their hands dirty with many members of society, Jesus always welcomed the prodigals of life into a relationship with him. Jesus delighted in spending time with them—be it on the street, at dinner, or at parties. It didn't matter who the person was, Jesus welcomed everyone—from tax collectors to prostitutes to those who were homeless. He even welcomed the religious leaders who came in secret to ask him questions. Rather than building walls to keep people out, Jesus removed the barriers that separated people from God. He didn't wait for them to clean themselves up first. He made the first move by welcoming them just as they were. For Jesus believed that his holy God absolutely delights in getting involved with real people.

One memorable story of how Jesus welcomed prodigals is his encounter with the woman at the well. Several aspects of that encounter offended even Jesus' own disciples:

✓ Jesus talked to a woman in a public place, which at that time was prohibited unless the woman was his wife—a big no-no, especially for one who claimed to be a religious leader.

✓ Jesus talked to a Samaritan—the despised enemy of the Jews.

✓ Jesus talked with a Samaritan woman who had been married five times and was now "living in sin" with a man.

In essence, Jesus defiled himself by welcoming a conversation with her. But in so doing he was able to remove the barriers between the two of them and in the process whet her appetite for and offer her the soul-satisfying water of eternal life.

How does your church make prodigals feel? Do you gladly receive them into your congregation? Are you willing to "get your hands dirty" with scandalous people?

Some time ago a Baptist pastor and friend of mine shared an experience with me. He had received a call from a couple who wanted their baby dedicated (a service performed by churches that subscribe to adults-only baptism). The couple wasn't married, and they weren't churchgoers. They had already called one church to set up the dedication and the pastor had agreed to perform this service on one condition: The father would not be allowed to attend the ceremony—only the mother! So the couple kept looking.

When this couple called my friend, he warmly welcomed them to come to his church and agreed to do the dedication. The couple is now actively involved in the congregation. Two things won them over: 1) the unconditional welcome they received from the pastor and the congregation, and 2) the fact that during the service the pastor wore a Cleveland Browns jersey. Upon seeing that shirt, the father knew he had found a place where he could belong.

In a previous book (*Unfinished Evangelism: More Than Getting Them in the Door*, Augsburg Fortress, 1995), I recount a conversation that bears repeating here. My mom had been hospitalized for several weeks with pancreatitis. My dad stayed at the hospital with her throughout the whole ordeal. At one point he headed to the waiting room to take a break. Another man, whose wife was also hospitalized for a prolonged period of time, had decided to do the same. As they sat in the waiting room together, the two men struck up a conversation. They talked about their wives, about their children, about their jobs, and eventually about their churches. The man said to my dad, "I'm a Lutheran. I go to a church down the street."

My dad replied, "Oh really! I'm a Lutheran, too. I go to Community Church of Joy. In fact, my son is one of the pastors there."

The man said, "I've heard about that church."

"Oh? What have you heard?" my dad asked.

"They're not really Lutheran."

"Well," my dad explained, "it is true that their worship styles are quite contemporary, but theologically they're very Lutheran."

"No, they're not Lutheran," the man said. "They let anyone in!"

Isn't that the point!

Is your church a place that welcomes anyone and everyone? Are you willing to build the kind of church that puts prodigals at ease so that they'll feel at home and eventually embrace the values of Christianity? Or will your church be a congregation for churched people only? Are you willing to remove the barriers that keep people out and that keep you separated from them? As one person put it: Some folks make you feel at home. Others make you wish you were. How does your church make prodigals feel? How do you want to make them feel?

3. Prodigal Hugging Churches Celebrate Culture (John 2:1-12)

Three days later Mary, the mother of Jesus, was at a wedding feast in the village of Cana in Galilee. Jesus and his disciples had also been invited and were there. (John 2:1-2 CEV)

One of Jesus' first miracles took place at a wedding. Imagine the scene: In Jesus' day, a wedding celebration could last up to a seven days, with wine flowing all week long. By the end of the week people were no doubt pretty loose after all of the wine and conversation.

And in the middle of it stands Jesus. His presence at the wedding shows that Jesus doesn't withdraw from or distance himself from culture. Instead he gets right in and celebrates with it. He even added to this particular celebration. When the week's worth of wine ran out, Jesus provided some more. And not just a little bit. He walked over to six jugs, each containing 20 to 30 gallons of water, and turned that water into wine, producing another 120 to 180 gallons of the stuff. The act was absolutely scandalous. On the one hand, what kind of religious leader brings his or her own bottle, let alone gallons and gallons of alcohol to a party? Even more scandalous, Jesus used the water set aside for spiritual purification and turned it into wine. He defiled water that was meant to ceremoniously cleanse people.

That miracle is still scandalous today. Many religious leaders desperately try to show that Jesus did not really turn the water into wine but into grape juice. They reason that Jesus surely wouldn't help people get drunk. (As someone who doesn't drink, who had a grandfather who was an alcoholic, and who, as a result, is pretty anti-alcohol because of all of the pain it causes people, I admit that I find this miracle particularly troublesome.)

The wedding at Cana, however, was not the only troublesome party that Jesus attended. If a party was being held in Galilee or Jerusalem, Jesus was sure to be there. Because these gatherings attracted what some might call the lowlife of society, most religious leaders stayed as far away as possible. But not Jesus. While he may not have always agreed with the lifestyles of the guests or the host, Jesus still enjoyed the people and the festivities, and in the process maintained his integrity.

In fact, it never ceases to amaze me just how at ease Jesus was with culture and how at ease culture seemed to be with him. For example, within hours of meeting Jesus, Matthew (a member of society's most hated profession—tax collectors) felt comfortable enough with this religious leader to invite Jesus to a party at his house—a party with a guest list consisting of notorious sinners (Mark 2:13-17). I don't know about you, but that's not the first place I would think of to invite an esteemed religious leader. Yet Matthew sensed something special in Jesus. He knew intuitively that Jesus would fit in with his friends and that they would feel comfortable around him as well. Jesus accepted them and they accepted him.

How comfortable do you feel around notorious sinners, even not so notorious ones? How comfortable are they around you? How at ease are our congregations in the presence of non-believers and how at ease are they in our places of worship?

Jesus often enjoyed spending time with people in their own environment because it was there that his light became more visible. It provided him the opportunity to bring the kingdom of God into the lives of others, be it through a relationship of unconditional

Later, Jesus and his disciples were having dinner at Levi's house. Many tax collectors and other sinners had become followers of Jesus, and they were also guests at the dinner.

(Mark 2:15 CEV)

acceptance and forgiveness (forgiving the "sinful" woman who washed Jesus' feet with her hair, tears, and expensive perfume at the dinner party hosted by Simon the Pharisee) or through bringing lasting joy to them (turning the water into wine—a symbol of joy —at the wedding in Cana).

Because of his actions however, Jesus was accused of being a drunkard and a glutton (Matthew 11:18-19). Scandalous stuff for a religious leader. I'm not sure many pastors could survive long in our congregations if such accusations were made of them.

Is your church willing to risk its reputation and be labeled a group of gluttonous, drunken, party animals? Would you wear that label as a badge of honor? I don't literally mean that we should promote that type of behavior—just as Jesus was never a glutton or a drunkard, nor did he ever condone such behavior. But is your church willing to welcome all members of society, even those people whose behavior might be offensive, so they can taste and see that the Lord is good? Are you willing to find the good in culture, or will you isolate yourself from the world?

My brother serves as a pastor in Canton, Ohio, and he celebrates culture as well as anyone I know. In just two years he's been able to build relationships with the movers and shakers of the city by offering his help in building a better community. He shares a prayer

right before the "Pro Football Hall of Fame" 10 kilometer race—
with more than 1,000 runners silently listening. He puts up signs on
the church property advertising citywide festivals, even though they
aren't "Christian events." He's hanging with the community. He's
being a presence of light. His church is learning how to celebrate
culture in order to show culture the love of Christ.

Taking his cue from Jesus, he's learned that not all of culture is
bad. When God created the world he called it good. In assuming the
form of culture in the person of Jesus, God celebrates culture. Can
we as a Church celebrate culture and be a presence in culture without condoning it and being absorbed by it? Will we celebrate culture
by using its music, its images, its language, in order to reach it? Are
you willing to be stigmatized as a gluttonous, drunkard church?
Take that one back to your church council next week!

4. Prodigal Hugging Churches Affirm Culture (Acts 17:16-34)

*People of Athens, I see that you are very religious. As I was going through
your city and looking at the things you worship, I found an altar with the
words, "To an Unknown God." You worship this God, but you don't really
know him. So I want to tell you about him.* (Acts 17:22-23 CEV)

One day the wind challenged the sun to a contest to prove that
it was more powerful than the sun. Looking down on an overcoat-
clad man walking along the road, the wind said, "Let's see who can
get that man to take off his coat." The sun was up to the challenge
and said, "It's a deal. You go first." The wind began to blow, gently
at first, and then it grew stronger and stronger, pushing against the
man. Finally, the wind was so strong that the man couldn't move
forward. Rather than blowing the coat off, however, the fierceness of
the wind only caused the man to wrap the coat tighter around his
body to fight off the cold.

After the wind had run out of energy, the sun took over, gently
warming the man. Soon the man was so warm and comfortable that
he took off his coat. As someone once wrote, "If you would win the
world, melt it, don't hammer it."

Paul used the sun's approach in Athens. As Paul stood on Mars Hill, he found himself surrounded by myriads of idols—different kinds of gods for different kinds of faith. In fact, there were so many gods in Athens that one Greek of the day remarked that it was easier to find a god than a person in the city. As Paul surveyed all of the idols, he was deeply disturbed in his spirit. As a Jew and a Christian, this blatant breaking of the First Commandment scandalized him.

Yet notice how Paul begins his discussions with the Greeks gathered around him. Rather than berating them for worshiping idols, rather than condemning them for choosing the wrong God, rather than antagonizing them for not getting it right, Paul affirms them. He warms them up to his message by patting them on the back for their great interest in spiritual matters. Although Paul completely disagrees with them, he chooses to build a bridge to them by affirming their common ground. Having warmed them up, he's able to point them to the true God.

> *God did not send his Son into the world to condemn its people. He sent him to save them!*
> (John 3:17 CEV)

As culture moves from *modernism* (the belief that reality is found in reason, science, and empirical data) to *postmodernism* (the belief that reality is found in experience), it increasingly looks like Paul's world. On Mars Hill, Paul found himself in the middle of the reason-based Stoics (the *moderns* of that time) and the experiential Epicureans (the "eat, drink, and be merry" *postmoderns* of that time), with hundreds of faith systems in between. And his handling of that situation gives us clues for how we can share Jesus in a similar culture.

As was true in Paul's day, starting with exclusionary, propositional truth statements no longer connects with culture today. Tolerance has become the new overarching value in society. The Church needs to understand that culture tolerates all forms of spirituality, except "exclusionary" faith systems. That means that in order to connect with today's postmodern culture we need, like Paul, to win the right to be heard. And that right to be heard begins with affirmation rather than condemnation.

Certainly, as Truth gets fuzzier and loses its capital T, we must increasingly and more articulately share the unique message of Jesus. But again, in order for culture to hear that unique message we need to start by affirming culture rather than blowing it away through the gale-force winds of "TRUTH."

Prodigal Hugging Churches use warmth rather than force, affirmation rather than condemnation, when trying to reach culture. They follow Jesus' example and lead with kindness.

A moving illustration of how Jesus leads with kindness is found in an encounter he had with an adulterous woman. One day a group of men brought to Jesus a woman who they claimed they had caught in the act of adultery. (As I read that story, three questions immediately come to my mind: What kind of religious people hang around tents where adultery is being committed? How long did they watch before deciding to take her to Jesus? Where was the man who was committing adultery with the woman?)

The men threw the woman down at Jesus' feet and said, "This woman has committed adultery. According to our laws she deserves death. What do you say?"

Jesus stooped down and wrote in the sand. He knew the woman was guilty. He knew she had done something very wrong and hurtful. He knew that the laws of the day demanded her death. But instead of waiting for her to confess her sin and repent, instead of condemning her and shaming her publicly, Jesus led with kindness. He looked the woman in the eyes and gently said, "I don't condemn you." And having warmed her heart with a word of grace, he was then able to begin the process of helping her become all God wanted her to be. Jesus said to the woman, "Go, and sin no more." As a result, her life was changed—not through a word of condemnation, but through a word of love and hope.

Paul says it this way: "Do you not realize that God's kindness is meant to lead you to repentance?" (Romans 2:4 NRSV). Another translation says: "Don't you know that the reason God is good to you is because he wants you to turn to him?" (CEV).

Notice what motivates repentance—or change—in our lives. Notice what comes first. It's not our decision to be different. It's not some word of condemnation or guilt. It's not our repentance that moves God to act in kindness toward us. What motivates a new direction in our lives is God's kindness. God uses goodness to draw us to a new way of living. God always makes the first move by reaching out to us with grace, by leading with kindness. And having won us over with his love, God then is able to gently begin the process of molding us into his image.

As author Leonard Sweet writes:

> A liquid, no matter how yielding and transient it appears, can erode stone. Soft water wins out over hard rock every time. When people call you a "softie" or a "soft touch," remember the power of water's "soft touch" to carve the Grand Canyon.

> Over time, there is nothing stronger than water. Water wears down even rock to make a new world. No matter how hardened and stony the human heart, softness defeats hardness . . . over time every time; gentleness beats rigidness . . . over time every time; fluidity overcomes flintiness . . . over time every time. The waters of abounding grace are even more powerful than death.

> — Leonard Sweet, *AquaChurch,* Group, 1999, p. 26

Many years ago two boys served as altar boys in the Catholic Church. Although they were born across the world from each other, one in Croatia and one in Illinois—their stories were somewhat similar. Both grew up in the Catholic Church. Both helped their priest serve communion. And coincidentally, both spilled the wine on the carpet—an accident that profoundly impacted both of them.

When the Croatian priest saw the spilled wine he slapped the boy across the face and said, "You clumsy oaf. Get out of here." That young boy grew up to be the atheist leader of Yugoslavia, Josip Broz Tito. The priest in Illinois, when he saw the spilled wine, knelt down, looked the boy in the eyes and said, "It's OK, son. You'll do a better job next time." That boy grew up to be Bishop Fulton J. Sheen, whose words and writings inspired millions of people.

Jesus works that same way. He dazzles people with love. While on earth, Jesus touched dirty, unclean lepers before they were healed. He ate with sinners and prostitutes before they left their pain-filled lifestyle. He always began with the unexpected act of acceptance and kindness, an act that motivated change. And he invites his Church to do the same.

When it comes to relating to culture, does your church offer the warm rays of the sun or the pounding, driving force of the wind? Does it use hammers and chisels or the soothing waters of God's grace? Does it lead with castor oil or does it offer the sweet tasting milk of God's kindness (2 Peter 2:2-3)? Does it affirm culture and move it to Jesus? How might you do more to affirm culture? Are you willing to risk the scandal it might cause?

5. Prodigal Hugging Churches Engage Culture (The Parables of Jesus)

Jesus used stories when he spoke to the people. In fact, he did not tell them anything without using stories. So God's promise came true, just as the prophet had said, "I will use stories to speak my message and to explain things that have been hidden since the creation of the world." (Matthew 13:34-35 CEV)

To *engage* means to attract and hold by influence and power, to induce to participate. Jesus was a master at attracting and holding the attention of an audience. He often engaged people by starting with culturally familiar symbols in order to lead his listeners to spiritual truths. He would call their attention to birds, or farmers, or mustard seeds, or pearls, and then talk about what those things teach about God's kingdom. On the surface, there was nothing particularly religious about the images used in his parables. The parables themselves seemed fairly entertaining and simple. But once engaged by the images, people were drawn into life-changing truths.

Some of the battle lines drawn in churches today have to do with secular and sacred holidays—particularly Halloween, Easter, and Christmas. Mentioning pumpkins or Santa or the Easter Bunny in church raises the blood pressure of many Christians. They fear that such references sell out or compromise the religious meaning of the holidays—or in the case of Halloween, focus on evil rather than God. In many ways I share their concern. At the same time, however, these "secular" images engage culture and capture their imaginations as they celebrate the various holidays.

I happen to be a huge Santa fan. I even collect Santas as mementos of my travels. Over the years, I've made various appearances at our church as Santa Claus and have tried to use that opportunity to have "Santa" tell kids the real story of Christmas. Every time I've done so, however, a few parents have expressed their concerns over Santa visiting our church, feeling that Santa detracted from the story of Jesus. Yet the reality is that Santa takes front and center in the hearts and minds of children every Christmas.

So one year I decided to preach a sermon about Santa called "Guess Who's Coming to Town?" Rather than condemning Santa as anti-Jesus and overly commercial, I shared my love for Santa. I told the story of how Santa came to be, starting with a boy named Nicolas, who gave gifts because of his love for Jesus. I shared a few of the legends concerning Nicolas and how he eventually became the Bishop of Myra. And I talked about how Nicolas ended up becoming what we now know today as Santa.

I spent the rest of the message comparing Santa and Jesus in three particular areas: 1) *Gift-giving*—how Santa's gifts don't last, whereas Jesus' gifts are eternal, 2) *Love*—how Santa's love is conditional whereas Jesus' love is unconditional, and 3) *Presence*—how Santa only comes once a year, whereas Jesus is a friend who will never leave us nor forsake us. The point was to engage the audience by starting with a well-known character, affirm that character, and then move to Jesus.

We tried something similar with Halloween. Halloween had become a divisive issue for some in our congregation. A few of our

ministries held annual Halloween parties, convinced that Halloween is nothing more than a night of fun, free candy, and community spirit. Others saw it differently, believing that any participation in
Halloween at any level is to participate in the evil, superstitious
roots of the holiday. Understandably, they were distressed by any
reference to Halloween in a church context. At the same time, most
people in the United States enjoy Halloween, look forward to it, and
participate in it.

In 1999, Halloween fell on a Sunday, and an overwhelming
number of people in the United States were thinking about trick-
or-treating that night. So we decided to engage people with that
culturally familiar and popular event in the hope of moving them
to spiritual truth. We used Halloween as a way to talk about
Christian decision-making, with Paul's discussion of idol meat in
1 Corinthians 8 to guide us. We themed the service "A Christian
Approach to Halloween." At the end of the worship experience, we
gave people the opportunity to do something constructive if they
decided to hand out candy that night. We printed up 25,000 orange
business cards that said, "This free candy is given as a reminder that
God loves you—no strings attached. If we can ever be of help please
call us." We listed our church name, address, and phone number on
the back of the card. (See Appendix B on pages 53–63 for the music,
message, and drama for this service.)

Philip Longfellow Anderson illustrates a unique approach to
engaging culture in his book of sermons entitled *The Gospel According to Disney* (Longfellow Publishing, 1999). Each sermon begins
with a discussion of an animated Disney film and then ties it to a
biblical text. For example, Longfellow uses the poison apple of
Snow White as a way to talk about the poison fruit of Eden and our
tendency to ingest these alluring but deadly pieces of fruit. He uses
Pinocchio to talk about honesty and the biblical view of what it
means to be human. By using culturally familiar images, Longfellow
engages culture and moves it to biblical truth.

One congregation sets aside the month of February to focus on
the family. Over four weekends they look at the subjects of raising

children, marriage, parenting teens, and singleness. Valentine's Day sets the agenda for the marriage weekend, and the rest flow from there. One year they used familiar TV families and shows to engage people around family issues—TV families like the Cleavers from *Leave It to Beaver*, TV couples like the Buchmans from *Mad About You*, and TV singles like the lead characters on *Seinfeld* and *The Mary Tyler Moore Show*. Using these familiar cultural images immediately draws people into the message.

In worship, small groups, classes, and seminars, we have an opportunity to engage people by starting with the familiar. The familiar might include stress, emptiness, guilt, consumerism, hopelessness, fear, a national or international event, a popular movie, song or TV show, or a special occasion like Valentine's Day. How can we use these everyday familiar images to engage people in order to lead them to the gospel?

In discussing the engaging of culture from the perspective of the religious community and rock music, author and columnist Michael Medved writes:

> With the entertainment industry as ubiquitous as it is, we can hardly feel surprised that the old religious community tactic of ignore-it-and-it-will-go-away has proven so singularly ineffective. Countless studies, and our own real-world experience, make clear that the isolation strategy won't work and can't work. That doesn't mean that people of faith should give up all objections and criticism and even confrontation with rock 'n roll reality; but it does mean that engagement is a far more appropriate approach than isolation.

> —from Mark Joseph, *The Rock and Roll Rebellion:*
> *Why People of Faith Abandoned Rock Music and Why They're Coming Back*,
> Broadman and Holman Publishers, 1999, p. xiv

Rather than isolating from or ignoring culture, Prodigal Hugging Churches look for ways to use familiar cultural icons, images, and symbols to move people to Christ. How might your church do a better of job of engaging culture?

6. Prodigal Hugging Churches Use Culture (John 9)

After Jesus said this, he spit on the ground. He made some mud and smeared it on the man's eyes. Then he said, "Go and wash off the mud in Siloam Pool." (John 9:6-7 CEV)

Of all of the characteristics of Prodigal Hugging Churches, I think "using culture" ranks at the top for scandal. At our leadership conferences, people increasingly ask us if there ever comes a point when the use of culture is too much—particularly in the area of technology. Does there come a time when all the video equipment and sound systems (with guitars and drums) shapes the gospel rather than the other way around?

John 9 records a fascinating story in which Jesus uses the stuff of culture to help a man in need. A blind man came to him for healing. Rather than simply touching the man and giving him sight, Jesus took some dirt, mixed it with his spit, and put it on the man's eyes. Two thousand years later, we read the story and simply scratch our heads wondering why Jesus added an extra step or two to the healing process. But two thousand years ago, according to some scholars, that extra step or two shocked the religious community, as people at that time viewed the combination of mud and spit as a sign of magic. Jesus opened himself up to real misunderstanding. Yet in so doing, he brought sight to the blind man.

The use of culture in the church always has been controversial and scandalous—in part because we fear that the gospel might be absorbed by or perverted by the cultural tools we use.

Leonard Sweet tells us that fierce objections followed every time the Bible was presented in a new technological form. For example, when the Bible moved from scrolls and parchment to print and book, Johannes Trithemius, the abbot of Sponheim, denounced the change, saying, "If writing is put on to parchment it can last for a thousand years, but how long will printing something on paper last? At the most a paper book could last for two hundred years" (Leonard Sweet, *AquaChurch*, Group, 1999, p. 62).

Sweet goes on to say that the use of the printing press divided Christians in the 16th century. It was highly controversial. Today, computers and the Internet are dividing the Christian world as we try to figure out what is and isn't appropriate in proclaiming the gospel. The use of culture always has been unsettling.

My brother forwarded an e-mail message to me that makes the point well. It reads in part:

> My boss once told me how, in the late 1950s and early 1960s, churches in New Orleans debated hotly (get it) whether they should install air conditioning. This may sound like a no-brainer today, but, at that time, air conditioning was relatively new to the masses, was terribly expensive, and frankly, just hadn't been done in the church. And believe me, for you folks in the more moderate climates, it is absolutely miserable down here in the summer. The traditionalists lamented that the cost would drive churches out of business and pointed out that our fathers, grandfathers, and great-grandfathers had worshiped without A/C and did just fine. Even worse, they feared people might slip into church, not for holy, righteous reasons, but merely for the cool air.

The fact is that the gospel has always been culturally bound. Every expression of Christianity uses technology somehow. From organs to hymnals, from indoor plumbing to heating systems, from flannel boards to fax machines, from crayons to computer programs, Christianity has always been and always will be bound to technology. Yet as technology continues to change and in the process reshapes the way we present the gospel, it will continue to be resisted by some as well. Many people will continue to warn us that too much technology will make Christianity in general and worship in particular too glitzy and too much like entertainment; that it will take our focus off of the gospel and dazzle us with technological toys. They'll try to convince us that technology dumbs-down worship.

And that's a real risk. But it's a risk worth taking. For God has always chosen to use culture to convey the gospel. From burning bushes to talking donkeys to bread and wine and water, God always uses the stuff of culture to redeem culture. God will use whatever tools are available. After all, isn't the use of human flesh as seen in the Incarnation the greatest, loving act of dumbing-down ever?

Over the last several years, a new sensory experience has emerged in popular culture—rhythm dancing. It can be seen in hit touring shows like *Lord of the Dance* and *Tap Dogs*. My favorite show is *Stomp*, in which the cast utilize their feet, hands, garbage cans, and even the kitchen sink to create rhythmic experiences.

A group of our teenagers at Community Church of Joy have been captivated by this new form of expression and created a *Stomp*–like group called Indecisive Rhythm. During major events, like our Christmas program, they put together a rhythmic routine that helps create a mood of celebration or that helps enhance the story (think the Little Drummer Boy on trash cans).

One year we decided to use the group to kick off our contemporary Christmas Eve services. With the house dark, the guys entered from the back, yelling, "Glory to God in the highest, and peace to all on whom his favor rests." Once they reached the stage, they celebrated the birth of the Savior through the "joyful noise" of rhythmic trash cans.

Two days prior to the service I received a call from a reporter for the *Arizona Republic,* our citywide newspaper. She was writing an article about how churches follow up with visitors after the Christmas holiday. We had spent about 40 minutes talking about marketing and how to get people to come back when she asked me what we were doing for Christmas Eve.

I explained that we had eight services: The first one geared to families, followed by three contemporary services, then two traditional services, and finally two acoustic experiences (guitars/keyboards without amplifiers, along with percussion instruments). When I mentioned that the contemporary services would start out with our *Stomp*–like group, the reporter stopped me and asked me what that meant. When I told her, she said, "Wow, my teenage daughter would love that. In fact, I think our readers would find that fascinating." She asked if we could get Indecisive Rhythm to pose for a picture the next night. She was hoping to run the story on Christmas Eve day and thought our rhythm group would make for an interesting spin on Christmas.

On Christmas Eve day, I ran out to pick up my newspaper, hoping to see the article in the regional section of the paper (the part that goes only to our side of town). To my surprise, a color photo of Indecisive Rhythm was on the front page of the *Arizona Republic*. The front page!

That day we received almost 300 phone calls asking about the services. That evening, at the start of the three contemporary services, the trash cans sat under dim lighting on the stage. As I stood in back before the first contemporary service, I heard one boy say to his mom when he saw the stage, "Hey, Mom, this is the trash-can church." Our attendance for the night was up by almost 2,000 people from the previous year, largely due to the coverage of our innovative use of culture to tell the story of Christmas.

We saw his true glory, the glory of the only Son of the Father. From him all the kindness and all the truth of God have come down to us.

(John 1:14 CEV)

Contrast that with the comment of one of our former members who months prior to Christmas Eve had complained about several of our uses of culture, like the use of video clips during the sermons. In one moment of anger and frustration he asked, "What do trash cans have to do with Jesus!?!"

I said it depends how they're used. In the case of our church, as the Christmas Eve service points out, they have everything to do with Jesus. In reality, the same question can be asked about pipe organs, or air-conditioners, or fellowship halls, or potlucks.

The truth is, cultural stuff isn't exclusively good or bad—it depends how it's used. TV can destroy or educate. Pipe organs can soothe us or frighten us. Brick and mortar can build cathedrals or houses of prostitution. Wine can make one drunk or convey the forgiveness of Jesus.

Prodigal Hugging Churches constantly look out for the latest technological advances that will help them further the kingdom of God. They seek to use the stuff of culture in order that culture might be redeemed. They also look to culture in order to learn from it that they might more effectively share the gospel.

Walt Kallestad, our senior pastor, has for years looked to the best in the business world, seeking insights, practices, and models that can help us build a more effective mission center. Some Christians find such "benchmarking" distasteful, arguing that the church is not a business and should not be impacted by business. Prodigal Hugging Churches see it differently. They want to learn from the best—from inside or outside of the Church—in order to impact the world with the gospel.

Walt's passion for learning from business, combined with my love and his love for Disneyland, led us to create a conference for church leaders called "The Imaginative Church." Held on the campus of the most imaginative place in the entire world, Walt Disney World, four hundred of us spent a few days sitting at the feet of a Disney trainer. We learned from her all we could about how to dream and how to treat our members and visitors as honored guests. No one does it better than Disney. We used the afternoon sessions to translate our learnings from Disney into a church setting. The conference far exceeded our best expectations.

It also, however, offended and angered a number of people. We received several vicious, hate-filled letters from Christians because we partnered with Disney. But as the four hundred who attended the conference discovered, we can learn from culture. Many businesses do a whole lot better than do many of our churches in treating people with dignity and respect. And Prodigal Hugging Churches aren't afraid to rub shoulders with culture in order to learn from it and then use that learning to try to impact culture with the love of Christ. Prodigal Hugging Churches listen to and use culture to help redeem culture.

7. Prodigal Hugging Churches Serve Culture (Philippians 2:1-11)

Let the same mind be in you that was in Christ Jesus, who, though he was in the form of God, did not regard equality with God as something to be exploited, but emptied himself, taking the form of a slave, being born in human likeness. (Philippians 2:5-7 NRSV)

I talked with a pastor some time ago who is trying to build a church that hugs prodigals. It hasn't been easy. Some in his church have been highly resistant. They struggle with the extent to which outside culture and those not affiliated with the church ought to influence the culture of the church.

As the pastor talked about the need to create a worship service more accessible to people who were not going to church, one of his leaders countered by saying, "Look, if you invite guests into your house you don't rearrange your furniture just because they tell you they don't like the way it is. In the same way, we can't let outsiders dictate the kind of music or the style of worship we offer just because they don't like it." In essence, that man was saying that culture must conform to us before we'll reach outsiders.

Two thousand years ago, God conformed himself to culture in order to reach it. In the person of Jesus, God laid aside his own rights and privileges and became like a slave. As radical as it sounds, God, who is deserving of our service, came to serve us in order to save us.

Prodigal Hugging Churches take their cue from the Incarnation and lay aside their own needs and agendas and put the needs of the prodigals ahead of their own. They go out of their way to listen to culture that they might more effectively share Jesus with culture in relevant ways. Offering a more culture-friendly worship service, getting out into the community, and performing free acts of kindness (like washing car windows, trimming bushes, and a host of other servant-oriented actions) enables us to hug the prodigals in our community and offer them the love of Christ. Prodigal Hugging Churches exist to serve culture in the name of Jesus.

Culture Encounter 3

Every December, Joy's performing arts team attempts to design a Christmas program that creatively tells the story of Christmas to a non-Christian audience. Most church programs tell the story for believers. We want to tell it for non-believers. In 1998, with the non-church-going crowd setting the agenda, we designed a program centered on the theme "Christmas through the Ages." In the first half of the show we looked at musical styles and artists from the 1940s to the 1990s, featuring such performers as Nat King Cole, the Beatles, the Beach Boys, the Carpenters, Michael Jackson, and even Wayne Newton. People dressed up as each of these musicians came out and performed a Christmas song in the style of their era. The second half of the show focused on the timelessness of the true story of Christmas—how Christmas bridges the generations and how, through Jesus, it can become a reality in our lives no matter what our age.

The purpose of the first half of the show was to engage the audience by using familiar icons and music to capture their hearts and stir up fond memories. In the second half, having warmed them up, we sought to move them to the true story of Christmas. Quite honestly, the positive response overwhelmed us. In fact, each night the audience grew in size. A number of non-church-goers were jazzed that a church was willing to offer the kind of show we did—an entertaining program that still conveyed a heartfelt, inspiring message. Several of our older congregation members came up with tears in their eyes after the first half because the music had enabled them to walk down memory lane. Since we were initially concerned that our older folks might find the music in the first half too aggressive and loud, their affirmation was a delight.

But there was another, equally significant response to the concert. Some of our members, simply put, were horrified. They were offended that we had Wayne Newton doing the "Jingle Bell Hustle" in church and that Michael Jackson sang in the altar area. Some said they shed tears of shame on our behalf. They were so upset with the first half that they didn't (or couldn't) hear the gospel in the second half. Nor were they willing to listen to our explanation of why we designed the program the way we did and how our target audience responded. For some people it was the beginning of the end, and they eventually left the church.

The Scandal of Hugging Prodigals

Two thousand years ago, God, in the person of Jesus, did the scandalous thing and hugged prodigals. Two thousand years later, God invites us, the Church, to do the same. It needs to be said, however, that such a philosophy toward culture is filled with danger. Part of the danger is found in the questions this particular approach to culture raises: *How do we clearly convey the counter-cultural, life-transforming values of the gospel while immersing ourselves in the culture outside of the church? How do we make sure we're not absorbed by culture?* These are important questions. But I'd like to suggest that they need to be answered from the perspective of prodigal hugging—that we try to answer the questions with the prodigals already within our embrace—rather than from our usual perspective of withdrawal from and condemnation of culture.

The larger danger with hugging prodigals, however, is that hugging the prodigal is a scandalous approach to culture. Just as Jesus was misunderstood, just as the father of the prodigal son was misunderstood, so when we as a church decide to hug prodigals we, too, will at times be misunderstood. Unfortunately, some of those who don't understand, some of the "older brother" types, will be people in our churches—our brothers and sisters in the faith. And often, their misunderstanding of or disagreement with the mission to hug prodigals can turn toxic, as was the case with the older brother when his father welcomed home the younger son. They'll express anger and outrage over new forms of worship, trash cans, wrestlers, secular songs, video clips in sermons, and so on. They'll accuse us of selling out to culture. They'll say that we've compromised the gospel—that we've watered-down or dumbed-down the message. They'll accuse us, as they did with Jesus, of being so much like culture that people can't tell us apart. As a result, many congregations will find themselves dealing with a great deal of tension as they wrestle with what it means to really be the church. But that's the risk—that's the danger of doing what Jesus does. When you follow Jesus, you will always scandalize someone, and sometimes the scandalized will be our brothers and sisters in the faith. And as many of you know, the fallout of such a commitment to mission can hurt, and hurt deeply. Some of us wear the scars to prove it.

Confessions of an Older Brother

Now, so you don't think that I have it out for "older brother" types, let me remind you that I am one. I'm the oldest of five children, and I am a stereotypical older brother. My natural bent favors fairness, righteousness, perfection, law, and order. As the older brother, I'm continually frustrated by those who don't get it right —by those whose scandalous lifestyles disqualify them from my acceptance. So I understand the concern of the older brother. I understand why he was so outraged by the behavior of his younger brother. I also understand why he was so enraged at the ease with which his father accepted the younger son home. Younger siblings always seem to get away with it! As my first-born daughter put it when she shared her opinion of prodigal son, "Oh, my poor little brother blew his entire inheritance while I'm here working myself to death being a loyal child. Boo hoo!"

I can relate to the older brother, too. I am one in birth order and, unfortunately, sometimes one in my faith. I've been the judgmental older brother who's taken shots at churches and leaders for what I believed was the selling out of the gospel.

At the same time, like many of you, I've been on the other end of an older sibling's anger, misunderstanding, and condemnation. And it's painful. You begin to doubt your call and the dreams God has placed in your heart. And if you let that pain sidetrack you, you can loose sight of your vision.

Who Sets the Agenda?

Please understand that God still loves the older siblings. In the parable, the father reaffirmed his love for his older son. That love didn't change despite the older brother's judgmental attitude. Older siblings, too, need God's love and grace. And I, for one, am an older brother who is profoundly grateful for that grace.

Having said that, however, we as Christians have an important decision to make when it comes to the mission of our congregations:

To whom will we listen? Whose voice will set the agenda for mission and ministry? Will we listen to the voices of the "older brother" both within our own hearts and within our congregation? Will we let those voices determine our mission? Or will we risk criticism and condemnation from some and build a church committed to hugging the prodigals?

Mark 3:1-6 records an encounter between Jesus and some of his religious enemies as Jesus seeks to heal a man with a deformed hand. As I prayed through that story one day, I imagined myself sitting in the back of the synagogue during the Sabbath as the event unfolded. I watched as Jesus noticed the man and how a look of compassion filled Jesus' eyes.

Jesus calls the man toward him. I suddenly feel the person next to me tense up. He whispers to the man seated next to him. I can tell they're angry about something. Jesus senses it, too. He turns to the men sitting next to me and asks them if it's legal to do good things like save lives on the Sabbath. He knows their answer. Rules are far more important than people.

The men sit anxiously in the back of the room waiting for Jesus to "break the law" by healing the man. But they refuse to speak. Then I see something I don't expect—Jesus is angry. It's a side of him that makes me uncomfortable. And yet as I pray and think about those in my life who've put religiosity before prodigals, who've built walls between the sacred and secular, I feel my own anger grow. I realize that my anger turns too easily to bitterness, and I find myself not responding out of kindness when around "older brother" types. I wonder if Jesus felt the same way I feel.

In the excellent prayer guide *Friendship with Jesus,* David L. Miller shares the insights he received while praying through this story:

> Jesus' accusers remain faceless to me, but I can feel their eyes pressing on the back of my skull. . . . When Jesus calls forward the man with a paralyzed hand, I motion for the accusers to come beside me, but the wave of my arm is really trying to say, "Come on, try to understand what's happening."

"What are you trying to do?" you ask, looking at me. . . . They keep you from participating in my joy."

Yet even you, Lord, seem confused and distracted by the people in the back of the room. . . .

"Do they bother you, even you?" I ask. "Yes," you answer, irritated at their disbelief. . . .

"I need to do better," you say. I'm startled. I've never before had the thought that you should do better, but I immediately feel less troubled by my repeated failures to keep my mind on doing the work and service you have given me to do.

I think of how I frequently expend more energy worrying about what others are thinking of me than on being myself. . . .

"Focus on the gift the Father has given you to share. . . . Questions and objections will come, and some will hate you because of me. You will be able to handle that when it arises. Only don't turn around to look at those who frustrate you and cause you pain when there are gifts to give and souls to heal. This only distracts you from being yourself. It steals your joy and obscures the kingdom."

> —David L. Miller, *Friendship with Jesus: A Way to Pray the Gospel of Mark,*
> Augsburg Fortress, 1999, pp. 144-145

God deeply loves the older siblings of the world. But his passion is to reach out and hug prodigals. The question is, Who will set the agenda in our churches? Whose voice will we listen to? Will we dance with culture or sit it out? The eternal destiny of the prodigals God loves hangs in the balance.

Doing What Jesus Does

Like most parents in the 1960s and early 1970s, mine resisted the encroachment of rock and roll into our home. Mom and Dad wouldn't allow us to buy rock albums. They did, however, try to compromise with our "need" for rock music by giving us any halfway decent contemporary Christian albums they could find.

But like most parents, mine discovered that rock and roll had too much power to resist. They finally cracked under the pressure and allowed us to buy a few "45" records.

I remember the very first "45" records we purchased. Among them was B.J. Thomas's mega-hit "Raindrops Keep Fallin' on My Head," from the movie *Butch Cassidy and the Sundance Kid*. Looking back, that song seems pretty tame compared to today's music. But as my parents feared, it eventually led to the harder stuff—like Barry Manilow and Kenny Rogers.

"In the same way there is more happiness in heaven because of one sinner who turns to God than over ninety-nine good people who don't need to."
—Jesus
(Luke 15:7 CEV)

One of the first full-length albums my brother bought featured B.J.'s greatest hits (to that point in his career). I can still picture the album cover. I can still picture myself listening to the record in my bedroom, on my little record player, pretending I was B.J. Something about his voice and singing style touched my soul and spirit.

In 1977, I was reintroduced to B.J. after the release of his first Contemporary Christian album, *Home Where I Belong*. B.J. had undergone a Paul-like conversion experience after years of battling drug addiction. His incredible singing talent and his experience in making hit records in the "secular world" made *Home Where I Belong* a landmark gospel album, bringing contemporary Christian music to a new level.

I heard him in concert in Tacoma, Washington, several months after the release of *Home Where I Belong*. The auditorium was packed with long-time B.J. fans and with new fans who had been won over by his Christian album. The concert was awesome, as B.J. sang hit song after hit song.

Then, in the middle of the concert, B.J. shared his testimony. He talked about the years of drug addiction. He talked about being estranged from his wife. He talked about almost dying on a flight from one Hawaiian island to another, only to wake up in a hospital bed with a Catholic nurse hovering over him. When he found out what had happened, he said to her, "I can't understand why I'm still alive." The nurse responded, "You would die. But God's got something for you to do."

He talked about going home to his wife, Gloria, who had become a Christian through some friends. He talked about his daughter praying in school that daddy would come home and how that day B.J. walked back into his house. And he talked about the dramatic experience he had several days later, when Jesus miraculously freed him from his drug addiction with no withdrawal symptoms at all.

The audience hung on his every word. He actually spoke about a half an hour or more. From there he sang some of his new Christian songs, and ended the evening with a few more of his pop hits. As I experienced that event, I was not only moved by the way B.J.'s singing touched my spirit, I was not only awed by his testimony and the fact that someone who had lived with so much pain was now healthy and whole, but I found myself thinking, "Here's a guy who has the platform to speak to people that most 'professional religious types' will never have. Because of his successful music career he can draw in all kinds of people, entertain them, and then, in a non-threatening way, simply tell his story of faith."

B.J.'s encounter with Jesus had essentially saved his life and his marriage. His gospel albums stayed at the top of the charts for unheard of weeks on end. He even enjoyed a pop hit during that time with "Don't Worry Baby." He was singing to sold-out auditoriums all across the country, performing his pop and country hits, sharing his faith story, and singing his gospel songs. A whole new audience embraced B.J. He seemed to be the artist many Christians had been praying for—one who could bridge the "secular" and "sacred" worlds.

But there was another equally significant response to B.J. Not long after he started adding his testimony and gospel music to his show, some of his fans began to express frustration. Not his "secular" fans, but his Christian fans. They began to heckle him while he performed his hit pop or mainstream songs, demanding that he sing only about Jesus. In one concert in Tulsa, thousands of people exited the auditorium before B.J. was into his fourth song. They left in disgust because he was singing "secular music."

Although B.J. continued to set records and win awards with his gospel albums, his Christian fans were increasingly disenchanted with his unwillingness to let go of his former music and become a Christian entertainer. Religious leaders even got into the act, trying to convince him to move exclusively into the Christian market. B.J. insisted that he was not a "Christian entertainer," but an entertainer who happened to be a Christian. He was proud of his pop career and saw it as a gift of God. B.J. simply didn't see the difference between what he did as an entertainer and what others in the secular field, like teachers, police officers, and firefighters do. They didn't stop doing the jobs God called them to do even though they worked in a "secular" environment. And B.J. felt called to stay in the pop business. That was his job and his love. He didn't want to give up the hope that God could use him in both the pop and Christian worlds.

Eventually, however, the pain became too much. The constant condemnation, heckling, and harassment by Christians caused him to withdraw from that judgmental environment and head to the safe, accepting, confines of country music. But even that transition was not easy. Christians wouldn't let him go without venting their anger. Some called him with death threats. Others piled up his gospel albums and fired shotguns at them. Still others broke the windows of Christian bookstores that continued to carry his gospel albums. His music was banned from Christian radio stations and Christian bookstores all across the United States. He was condemned and written off as a backslider.

When asked if any of his Christian friends stood by him during that time, B.J. replied, "Man, not a one!"

One of his band members, in speaking about those tough years, said of Christians, "They made me feel so bad about myself."

Recently, I had a chance to hear B.J. perform at a Vegas Casino. (He once told me, "I can go in a casino and do five or six gospel songs back to back. . . . Some of the people will be drunk. They'll be smoking cigarettes and may be there with somebody else's wife. But there will be a total acceptance of what I'm doing. Then I can go in front of 'God's people' and sing "Hooked on a Feeling" and they will go up the wall. I've gotten to the point where I really love the people in the casinos who like gospel music . . .") I sat at a table with six people. The "older brother" in me surveyed the audience, particularly those next to me, and concluded that they probably weren't churchgoers. As always, B.J. put on a great show. And, as always, in the middle of the show B.J. asked if anyone wanted to hear some gospel music. Unlike the concerts when he first entered the Christian market, B.J. no longer shares his testimony. The years of pain have stayed with him, and he feels the need to distance himself from the Christianity he experienced. But he still sings about Jesus.

As B.J. sang "Amazing Grace," something happened in the casino showroom. I looked around and saw people all over the theater wiping their eyes. God was touching people in that setting through the use of an old hymn sung by a man for whom amazing grace was a life-changing experience. The prodigal continues to sing for other prodigals. As an evangelist at heart, I sat back in redeemed jealousy. I'd give my right arm for a chance to share my heart and faith like that with that kind of audience.

B.J. often opens his gospel segment with the song "Would They Love Him Down in Shreveport." The song asks several questions: "If they saw him riding in, long hair flying in the wind, would they love him down in Shreveport today?" The song goes on to ask us how we would respond today to someone who speaks with ease to junkies, whores, and thieves. To someone who tells us to turn the other cheeck and forgive those who have harmed us.

I've often wondered why B.J. chooses that particular song to open his gospel segment. My gut feeling, knowing what he went through back in the late 1970s and early 1980s, is that B.J. is trying to say that he's going to keep doing what Jesus does. Just as Jesus scandalized some by hanging out with the wrong kinds of people and doing things that made the religious uncomfortable, so B.J. will continue to do the same.

Will your church go and do likewise? Are you willing to do what Jesus does? Are you willing to risk the scandal and the wrath of the older siblings to touch prodigals?

In the biblical story, the father scandalized himself for the sake of his prodigal son. Jesus scandalized himself for our sake and the sake of all the prodigals like us. Every day he lifts his robes and runs to us that we might experience his embrace and love. And he invites us to do the same for those who don't know him yet. He invites us to join him in the scandalous, daring, and exciting adventure of building a congregation that runs to culture and embraces, welcomes, and serves it that our communities might discover the life-transforming love of Christ.

The day I left home I knew I'd broken his heart
And I wondered then if things could ever be the same
Then one night I remembered his love for me
And down that dusty road ahead I could see
It was the only time I ever saw him run
And then he ran to me, took me in his arms
Held my head to his chest
Said, "My son's come home again"
Lifted my face, wiped the tears from my eyes
With forgiveness in his voice
He said, "Son, do you know I still love you?"
He caught me by surprise and brought me to my knees
When God ran, I saw him run to me.

Appendix A

The Prodigal Hugging Church Survey

Use the following survey to evaluate your church and ministry in light of the seven characteristics of a Prodigal Hugging Church (described on pages 19 to 39). You might choose to use this survey as part of a class, during a retreat, or at a board meeting. As you walk through these questions, prayfully ask God to show you how your congregation can more effectively reach out to those in your community not connected to Christ.

1. Embracing Culture

- In what ways does your church embrace culture or take on the form of culture? How does this cause stress and scandal in your church?

- How does your congregation slip into the "older brother" syndrome and shun culture? What are the unwritten rules that keep prodigals out?

- What two imaginative things can you do to embrace culture in the next six months?

2. Welcoming Culture

- How does your church make prodigals feel? How do you want them to feel? In what ways does your church antagonize prodigals—subtly or not so subtly telling them that they have to come to you on your terms, that they have to accept you as you are rather than the other way around?

- What are three daring and potentially scandalous things you can do in the next six months to help build a church where prodigals feel at home?

3. Celebrating Culture

- How would your congregation react if next Sunday the pastor stood in the pulpit and said, "God is calling us to be a church that wears the label—'glutton and drunkard'—as a badge of honor"? How might you help your congregation see this as a good thing?

- In what ways is your church a celebrating presence of light in the local culture? In what ways does your worship service celebrate culture?

- Dream of two ways to celebrate culture in the next six months (either in the worship service or by going into the community).

4.–5. Affirming and Engaging Culture

- Is your church a *water* church or a *hammer* church? Think of concrete examples of both.

- What two things might you do creatively to affirm culture in order to move it to Jesus?

- What two new ideas might you implement to more effectively engage culture during your worship services, small groups, or Bible studies?

6. Using Culture

- What uses of contemporary culture (including technology and the media) does your congregation currently use to carry out ministry? What modern-day uses of culture would scandalize some members of your congregation?

- When it comes to worship, does your service reflect the culture and technology of the 16th century? The 18th century? 1950s? The 21st century?

- What can you do in the next six months to become more connected to the 21st century?

7. Serving Culture

- In what ways does your church actively serve culture? In what ways does it boycott culture?

- What are two imaginative ways your church can serve culture in the next six months?

Evaluating the Risks

- Interacting with culture the way Jesus did is filled with risks and dangers. The first risk is the potential of alienating, angering, and scandalizing faithful church members. As you move toward becoming a Prodigal Hugging Church, how will you love and care for the "older siblings"?

- The other risk is subtler. In our attempts to embrace, welcome, celebrate, affirm, engage, use, and serve culture, we risk losing ourselves through condoning culture, being absorbed by it, or by being tainted by its values. Think of five practical ways to keep your church rooted in the counter-cultural values of the kingdom as you seek to do what Jesus did and immerse your congregation in culture in order that God might transform culture. How can you keep your eyes fixed on God's light while you stand in the darkness?

Evaluating Your Mission

- How will you know you have become a Prodigal Hugging Church? What indicators, feelings, and images will show that your congregation has joined the scandalous, life-transforming mission of Jesus?

Appendix B

A Prodigal Hugging Church Service

The following is adapted from the service held at Community Church of Joy on October 31, 1999. This service uses a video clip, worship choruses, a drama, and special music to build a cohesive, themed experience. The intent was to engage people by using a culturally familiar event, in this case Halloween, to move people to the gospel. The sermon was designed to reach people visiting church for the first time, as well as Christians who struggle with the issue of Halloween and Christian decision-making in general. It goes without saying that devoting Reformation Sunday to the topic of Halloween was considered a scandalous approach to mission by some people.

A Christian Approach to Halloween
1 Corinthians 8:1-8

Opener
Love Can Make it Happen
Music by Morris "Butch" Stewart, Words by Brenda Blonski,
Brenda Mitchell Stewart and Morris "Butch" Stewart, Hit Tunes Publishing Co., 1990
From the CD *Love's Still Changing Hearts* by the Imperials

Video Clip
It's the Great Pumpkin, Charlie Brown
(the scene where the kids are out trick-or-treating
and Charlie Brown keeps getting rocks)

Welcome
This weekend millions of children and adults will celebrate the second most popular holiday in the United States next to Christmas. They will dress up in costumes, some as their favorite super heroes, others as Disney characters, and still others as ghosts and witches. Many children will go from door to door in their

neighborhoods asking for free candy. Many teenagers and adults will attend parties with lots of games and food. When all is said and done, as a nation we will have spent $2.5 billion on Halloween.

Many of those who go trick-or-treating this weekend will be Christians. Like other Americans, they look forward to this one night when they can let down their hair down, so to speak, dress up like someone else, and get some free candy. They see it simply as a night to have some clean, innocent fun.

But there will be other Christians who choose to skip all the festivities. They don't see Halloween as innocent fun. They see it as a night devoted to evil and its forces. And they can't see any reason why a Christian would want to participate in such a night.

So who's right? Should Christians participate in Halloween? What does the Bible have to say about it? The bigger question is this, "How do we as Christians make wise, faith-based decisions when there are no clear yes-or-no, right-or-wrong answers?" That's what we're going to focus on today. Because Halloween is such a big deal in our culture, we're going to use it as an illustration for how to make decisions on those seemingly gray areas in life. So today, through the music, the drama, and the message, we want to look at Halloween from a Christian perspective—and more specifically, look at wise decision-making from a Christian perspective.

Worship Choruses

Your People Sing Praises
Russell Frager, Hillsongs Australia, 1995

Longin' for Your Touch
Paul Iannuzzelli, Living Stones Music, 1993

He Is Able
Rory Noland and Greg Furguson, Maranatha! Music, 1989

When I was kid I eagerly looked forward to Halloween. I could hardly wait to get my hands and teeth on all of that free candy. And every year, like other kids, I thought long and hard about who

I wanted to be on Halloween night. Because on that one night of the year I could be anyone I wanted to be.

Usually we would go down two or three blocks in our neighborhood and collect as much candy as we could. After hitting the neighborhood, we would hop in the car and head to Grandma's house. She always had an extra treat for us, like a box of Cracker Jack or a big Hershey bar.

Some of my best memories with my own children come from our evening walks on Halloween. Strolling through the neighborhood on a cool Phoenix night with my kids was one of the most relaxing, enjoyable times we spent together. And it was always so much fun dreaming up costumes for them, and sneaking candy from their hidden stash. I've always enjoyed Halloween night. I've always seen it as a night of fun, imagination, and, best of all, free candy.

But then, a few years ago, I had a few parents here at Joy question whether or not Christians should participate in Halloween. Quite honestly, even though I'm a pastor, the thought never crossed my mind before. As I said, I see Halloween as a fun, innocent night for neighbors to do something nice for each other. But these parents wondered how I, as a pastor, could celebrate a night supposedly devoted to Satan? And I have to admit, it's a fair question.

At the risk of boring you with a brief history lesson, Halloween traces its roots back to the religious superstitions of the Celts almost two thousand years ago. The Celts believed that the line between the living and the dead blurred on October 31, a pivotal night in their world marking the end of the summer and the beginning of winter. They were convinced that the ghosts of the dead returned on that night to cause trouble and damage their crops. They also believed the presence of these ghosts enabled their priests, called druids, to see into the future. So the druids would dress in costumes and give their prophecies.

By A.D. 43, the Romans had conquered Celt territory and absorbed Celt festivals into their own unique holidays. The Romans used October 31 to commemorate their dead and to honor the goddess of fruit and trees, Pomona. The symbol for Pomona is the apple, and this was probably the inspiration behind bobbing for apples on Halloween.

When Christianity spread into Celtic lands in the 800s, Halloween changed again. Pope Boniface IV designated November 1 as All Saints' Day to honor Christians saints and martyrs. Many people believed he was trying to replace the Celt festival of Halloween with a Christian one. Centuries later, when Europeans immigrated to North America, they brought the ever-evolving celebration of Halloween with them. While they kept many of the traditions, they downplayed the religious superstitions tied to those traditions making Halloween primarily a secular festival.

One of the traditions brought over from Europe was the use of costumes. Hundreds of years ago, when the dark of winter was an uncertain, frightening time, people were afraid to venture out in the dark. On Halloween, in particular, it was believed that ghosts came back to the earth to haunt people who left the security of their homes. So to avoid being recognized by ghosts on Halloween, people wore masks, hoping the ghosts would think they were fellow spirits. Another of those traditions was trick-or-treating, which started in England and Ireland when the poor would beg for food during Halloween festivities.

Although many of the traditions grew out of religious superstitions, Halloween has become an increasingly secular holiday for most Americans—a chance to have some fun and do something nice as a community. But, admittedly, that doesn't change the fact that Halloween was birthed out of religious superstition. And the holiday still has vestiges of that superstition attached to it—as seen in depictions of ghosts, black cats, and witches.

So what do Christians do with Halloween? Since Halloween is now a mostly secular event, can Christians trick-or-treat with a clear conscience? Or should we refuse to participate in something that has its roots in the superstitious? After all, aren't we really participating in that superstitious behavior when we put on the costume and trick-or-treat?

Almost two thousand years ago, one of the early leaders of the Christian Church faced a similar situation. The apostle Paul was confronted with an issue that was dividing the young church in Corinth, Greece. The issue had to do with meat, a portion of which had been used for idol worship, and the rest of which was cooked for dinner. Some Christians believed they could eat the meat without any hang-ups because they knew idols were nothing but pieces of wood and metal anyway. But other Christians were deeply troubled by the issue. They wondered how any Christian could eat such meat, fearing that by so doing they were participating in idol worship. Sounds fairly similar to our issue of Halloween, doesn't it?

Here is part of what Paul has to say to the Christians in Corinth concerning that issue:

> In your letter you asked me about food offered to idols. All of us know something about this subject. But knowledge makes us proud of ourselves, while love makes us helpful to others. In fact, people who think they know so much don't know anything at all. But God has no doubts about who loves him.
>
> Even though food is offered to idols, we know that none of the idols in this world are alive. After all, there is only one God. Many things in heaven and on earth are called gods and lords, but none of them really are gods or lords. We have only one God, and he is the Father. He created everything, and we live for him. Jesus Christ is our only Lord. Everything was made by him, and by him life was given to us.
>
> Not everyone knows these things. In fact, many people have grown up with the belief that idols have life in them. So when they eat meat offered to idols, they are bothered by a weak conscience. But food doesn't bring us any closer to God. We are no worse off if we don't eat, and we are no better off if we do.
>
> —1 Corinthians 8:1-8 CEV

We're going to take a few minutes today to look at how Paul helps the Corinthians answer their idol meat issue and how his advice can help us with the issue of Halloween and other subjects not specifically addressed by the Bible. But before we talk about it, let's pray together.

Special Music
In the Light
Charlie Peacock, Sparrow Song and Andi Beat Goes On Music, 1991
From the CD *Jesus Freak* by dc Talk.

Drama
Common Ground
by Brad Kindall
Copyright © 1999 Community Church of Joy. Used by permission.

Characters:	Lori
	Kim
	Jack (Lori's 8-year-old son)
Setting:	Lori's kitchen
Props:	table, chairs, coffeepot, coffee mugs, Jack's Halloween costume

Lori: *(Enters with coffeepot.)* Here we go. *(Lori pours coffee for Kim.)*

Kim: This is so nice of you.

Lori: I remember what it was like when we first moved in. You want to find some friends for your kids, but you don't know their parents, and it's hard to just walk up to someone's door and introduce yourself.

Kim: Yeah, and every neighborhood has their own rules about what's appropriate. Like, does the mom call and ask if it's OK for the kids to come over, or do the kids just walk over and knock on the door?

Lori: Oh, just knock on the door. We're very laid back around here.

Kim: Oh, I'm so glad.

(Lori's son Jack walks in wearing a costume.)

Jack: Trick or treat!

Lori: Well, look who's here. I think there are some suckers in the pantry. Go grab some and share them with the kids in the other room.

Kim: Cute costume.

Lori: Hey, why don't we get the kids together and go trick-or-treating together?

Kim: Oh, sorry, we don't celebrate Halloween.

Lori: *(pause)* What?

Kim: We just don't make a big deal of it.

Lori: You don't celebrate Halloween?

Kim: No. As we looked at the holiday and its origins in the occult, we felt like it was something we'd rather not have our kids involved in.

Lori: The occult? Well, we're not involved in the occult.

Kim: Oh, I'm not saying you are. Please don't misunderstand me.

Lori: I mean, Jack's only 8 years old. He just likes the candy.

Kim: Oh, I'm sure . . .

Lori: We go with him around the neighborhood. There's no way he could do any animal sacrifices. We're with him all the time.

Kim: I know, but I read that Halloween is the most active night of the year for satanic practices.

Lori: Well, I don't know about that stuff. It's just a family holiday around here. *(pause)* How do you feel about Arbor Day?

Kim: All for it.

Lori: Groundhog Day?

Kim: Sure.

Lori: St. Patrick's Day?

Kim: I'll be in green.

Lori: But no Halloween?

Kim: Sorry.

Lori: Hmmm . . . So do you think I'm doing damage to my kids by letting them trick-or-treat?

Kim: All I'm saying is that it's not for us. We just don't feel it's right to glorify the dark side.

Lori: I don't think we're glorifying the dark side.

Kim: Oh, of course not.

Lori: So, what does your family do on Halloween?

Kim: We usually rent a movie. I know! Why don't you come over after you go trick-or-treating?

Lori: What is the movie rated?

Kim: PG-13.

Lori: Sorry, but we have a hard-and-fast rule the kids can only see G-rated movies. Is there something else we could do?

Kim: Well, our kids have some video games?

Lori: Do they involve guns?

Kim: Well, yeah, a couple of them do.

Lori: We don't let our kids have anything to do with guns.

Kim: Maybe we could just have a barbecue.

Lori: We're vegetarians.

Kim: How can you survive without meat?

Lori: How can you kill a defenseless animal?

Kim: *(pause)* Wow, I wonder if we have anything in common.

Lori: Yeah, it's kind of weird.

(They sigh.)

Kim: What are your thoughts on Jesus Christ?

Lori: *(hesitant)* I'm . . . crazy about him.

Kim: Well, I am, too.

Lori: Well, that's something.

Kim: Yeah, it's a big something.

(They banter as lights fade.)

Every day Christians are confronted with decisions that don't necessarily come with simple yes-or-no, good-or-bad answers. Decisions upon which Christians don't necessarily always agree, decisions that aren't specifically spelled out in the Bible, decisions like what to do with the celebration of Halloween.

In Corinth, the issue was whether or not people should eat meat sacrificed to idols. The challenge was that Christians might not always know whether or not the meat they were buying at the local market had been included in a sacrifice. Only a portion of the meat was sacrificed and the rest was sold as food. So a Christian could end up eating idol meat without knowing it.

One group of Corinthian Christians was so sure of their faith in God that they were able to eat meat sacrificed to idols with a clear conscience and a satisfied belly. The other group of Christians knew intellectually that idols don't really exist, but that wasn't the point. They used to be idol worshipers, and it bothered them to eat something that was meant to honor another god, even if that god does not really exist.

The apostle Paul jumps headfirst into the debate and offers his perspective. But it's not quite the answer we'd expect. For rather than giving a yes-or-no answer, Paul offers some spiritual principles to help us make up our minds when it comes to the gray issues of life. And as we focus specifically on Halloween, I'd like to share four of those principles with you so that you can better come to your own decision.

First of all, Paul reminds us that Christianity is always about what God is for, not what God is against. Unfortunately, too much of Christianity has been expressed in terms of *don'ts*, which often rob us of joy and restrict life. But Christianity tells us that God is for us and that God is for life. God values anything positive that leads to joy, peace, and celebration.

We see that commitment to joy and celebration in the life of Jesus. Jesus loved life, and he loved being where life was happening. If there was a party in Jerusalem, Jesus was usually there. And the parties Jesus attended weren't necessarily the kinds of parties that religious leaders attended, because the "low life" of society often made up the bulk of the guest list. But that didn't stop Jesus. He took advantage of any celebration that was healthy, life-affirming, and joy-filled, even if it wasn't particularly religious. And where Jesus might not always agree with the lifestyle of the party host, he still enjoyed the people and the festivities without compromising his integrity. Jesus shows us that God is no killjoy; that God delights in anything positive, healthy, and affirming that brings delight to our hearts. Jesus shows us that God enjoys fun. And he invites us to do the same.

Second, the apostle Paul says that our decisions in life should always be made in the context of Christ's love for us and our love for him. Any great relationship is built not on rules, but on love. And when we love someone, we make decisions that reflect that love and bring honor to the person. When it comes to the gray areas of life, Paul encourages us to ask, "Will my actions honor Christ? Do they reflect his character? Do they reflect his commitment to joy and freedom?"

Third, Paul says that not only are we free to enjoy life, not only do we have the privilege of making decisions that honor Christ, but as Christians we are also free to act responsibly. When it comes to idol meat, Paul says clearly that there is absolutely nothing wrong with eating it. Idols don't exist anyway, so eat the meat and enjoy it. And if it bothers you, don't ask where the meat came from. Ultimately the meat is God's gift to us and is meant to be enjoyed.

Even though Paul sees nothing wrong with eating idol meat, and even though he seems a bit frustrated with those who do think there's something wrong with it, Paul says that Christians will always act out of a responsible love. He says that if his eating of idol meat will bother a more sensitive Christian, then he won't eat it. For Paul, his love for his brother and sister Christians is more important than his insights into his freedom in Christ.

Just as in Paul's day there were many people who saw nothing wrong with eating idol meat because idols don't exist, many people today see Halloween not as a celebration of evil but as a secular holiday that enables communities to do something nice for each other.

And yet, just as there were people in Paul's day who were troubled by the eating of idol meat, so there are people today who are troubled by Halloween. And if your celebration of Halloween will weaken or upset the young faith of a friend, Paul would encourage you to think twice before participating in the holiday—out of love for your friend. The faith development of your friend is far more important than Halloween.

Finally, Paul encourages us to look for a positive way to make a difference. That's always what Christianity has been about. In the 800s the Christian Church turned a holiday driven by superstition into a celebration of the Christians who have gone before us. In fact, many of the symbols of Christmas, like the Christmas tree, were once pagan symbols but now are reinterpreted in light of the gospel.

If you're going to celebrate Halloween, then do it in a way that reflects your faith. Stay away from those things that represent super-stitions and evil. Instead, dress up in costumes that are harmless, positive, and innovative. Make trick-or-treating not only a time to give free candy, but a time to offer a free reminder of God's love.

So, in light of Paul's principles, should Christians celebrate Halloween? On this issue, quite honestly, there is no clear yes-or-no answer. The good news is that the gospel allows each of us to decide according to our understanding of Jesus. So should you celebrate Halloween? What does your heart say? What does your under-standing of God say? And once you've figured it out, Paul would encourage you to feel good about your decision and to refrain from judging negatively anyone who would decide otherwise. For in Christ, on this issue, we're free either way.

But before you can make that decision, you need to know per-sonally this one who sets you free, who created you to enjoy life, who created you to celebrate. And if you don't know the freedom Christ gives, I'd encourage you today to meet him and enjoy the life, joy, and hope that he gives. For he is the sweetest, most satis-fying treat you'll ever experience.

Offering

Special Music
Hold on to the Cross
Leonard Ahlstrom, Eddie Carswell, Russ Lee, Sunday Shoes, 1997
From the CD *Love Revolution* by Newsong

Closing/Benediction

Other books by Joy Resources
and Community Church of Joy authors

Unfinished Evangelism:
More Than Getting Them in the Door
by Tim Wright
Augsburg Fortress, ISBN 0-8066-2794-8

Discover Jesus
by Ginny Wheeler
Joy Resources, ISBN 0-8066-4095-2

Discover the Bible
by Ginny Wheeler
Joy Resources, ISBN 0-8066-4096-0

Vital Christianity: A Seeker's Resource
by Ginny Wheeler
Joy Resources, ISBN 0-8066-4094-4

Christian Faith: The Basics
by Walt Kallestad
Augsburg Fortress, ISBN 0-8066-3397-2

The Everyday, Anytime Guide to Prayer
by Walter Kallestad
Augsburg Fortress, ISBN 0-8066-2796-4

Turn Your Church Inside Out:
Building a Community for Others
by Walt Kallestad
Augsburg Fortress, 0-8066-4034-0

Order through **www.augsburgfortress.org** or call **1-800-328-4648**.

For more information about Community Church of Joy,
visit **www.joyonline.org** and **www.joylead.org**.